THE ELVES
and
THE SHOEMAKERS

Retold and Illustrated by

J A D A   R O W L A N D

D1573375

A CALICO BOOK
Published by Contemporary Books, Inc.
CHICAGO · NEW YORK

With love for David and Sparks and, of course, Tommy

Library of Congress Cataloging-in-Publication Data

rowland, jada.
The elves and the shoemakers / retold and illustrated by
jada rowland.
p. cm.
Adaptation of: Die Wichtelmänner.
"A Calico book."
Summary: A poor shoemaker becomes successful with the
help of two elves who finish his shoes during the night.
ISBN 0-8092-4355-5
[1. Fairy tales. 2. Folklore—Germany.]
I. Wichtelmänner. II. Title.
PZ8.R792E1 1989
398.2'1'0943—dc19 88-34457
CIP
AC

Published by Contemporary Books, Inc.
180 North Michigan Avenue, Chicago, Illinois 60601
Manufactured in the United States of America
Library of Congress Catalog Card Number: 88-34457
International Standard Book Number: 0-8092-4355-5

Published simultaneously in Canada by Beaverbooks, Ltd.
195 Allstate Parkway, Valleywood Business Park
Markham, Ontario L3R 4T8 Canada

As the dull red sun slipped behind the gray factory rooftops of Lancashire, England, Timothy Sparks closed the shutters of Sparks' Shoeshop on Limpkin Lane. No customers again today.

His last sale had been a fortnight ago. He had made a pair of rough boots for one of the workers at the Tottenham mine. When the soot-covered miner had come to pick up his order, he had sneered, "Not near as neat a fit as the factory-made boots."

Timothy had been afraid that the miner wouldn't buy the boots after all, so he had reduced the price until it barely covered the cost of the leather.

The three bob he had received had gone to pay Doctor Pennyworth for the cough medicine his dear wife, Elizabeth, needed.

The money spent and the rent past due, Timothy worried to himself. Landlord Whipsnade would be coming again on Friday. It would be Timothy's last chance to pay up.

Well, there's leather enough for one more pair of shoes, thought Timothy. So, after cooking up some gruel and biscuits for supper, he made Elizabeth as comfortable as he could in their cramped living quarters above the shop. Then he sat down at his workbench to cut out the leather.

Without Elizabeth working beside him, it took him until midnight to finish. Tired though he was, Timothy didn't neglect his nightly ritual of setting out some new biscuit crumbs and a fresh thimbleful of raspberry wine, replacing what he had put out the night before. Timothy sighed, "For the luck of the Little People."

Timothy and Elizabeth, like many in England in those days, believed there were tiny Elves and Pixies and all manner of Faeries living in the towns and villages alongside human beings. But these Little People were almost never seen. It was rumored that these Wee Folk, being very mischievous, could cause a lot of trouble. But if one were careful always to leave a few leftover bits of food out at night, the Little People might bring great good fortune.

They never seemed to visit Sparks' Shoeshop, but Timothy spread out the crumbs anyway. Then, snuffing out the candle, he trudged up the stairs and went to bed.

But sleep did not come easily. How could he compete with those new machines that made shoes faster and more cheaply

than the best cobblers in England? Where would his little
family go if the landlord evicted them two days hence?
Timothy tossed and turned and finally fell into a fitful
slumber.

The next morning, Elizabeth shook a groggy Timothy
awake. He had overslept!

"Oh dear, oh dear," he cried. "I won't be able to finish the boots in time to put them in the shop window before the miners go by on their way to work."

Elizabeth tried to calm him. "Timothy, I feel much better today. I'll come back to work." But as she sat up, she began coughing again.

"No, no, dear Lizzie, you must rest. If I work quickly, I shall have the boots done before the morning shift is over at the mine."

Timothy dragged on his clothes and stumbled bleary-eyed down the narrow staircase to the shop. He shook down the ashes and shoveled new coal into the potbellied stove and then opened the shutters of the tiny window over his workbench.

As his eyes adjusted to the daylight, he drew back with a start. The leather was gone! The soles, the uppers, even the extra snippets of patent leather he had tacked to the wall had all vanished.

"Oh, no!" he cried with alarm. "Now we are surely ruined. It must be here somewhere." Looking about frantically, his eyes fell on the tacking bench and he stopped short. Neatly arrayed at the end of the bench were two boots more beautiful than any he had ever seen—a pair of size-five lady's walking boots, perfect from their patent-leather toes to their well-turned heels.

Timothy was dumbfounded. He looked about for some clue to this mystery. He searched the workroom, then the storefront, and even the cellar. But except for the leather, it seemed everything was just as he had left it the night before.

He returned to the shop and gingerly picked up the mysterious boots. Turning them over, he examined the precise tacking on the soles and squinted at the tiny stitches on the toe caps. Remarkable work! Still half-dazed and clutching the boots, Timothy wandered into the front of the shop. Realizing the display window was empty, he carefully placed the beautiful boots on the shelf. Then he went upstairs to tell Elizabeth of the mystery.

Now, it just so happened that on that very morning Squire

John Higginbottom III, owner of the Lancashire coal mines, was striding down Limpkin Lane on his way to the bank. As he passed Sparks' Shoeshop, the newly made boots caught his eye. He'd never noticed the shabby shop before, but the particularly fine stitching and carefully shaped uppers of these elegant boots were just what his wife, Abigail, had been looking for.

The Squire stepped briskly into the little shop and, tapping his stick sharply on the floor three times, called out, "Hullo, is anyone about?"

Timothy clattered down the staircase and emerged from behind the curtain. When he saw the elegant dress of the Squire, he blinked twice. This was not one of his usual customers.

"I say there, that is an uncommonly fine pair of boots in the window," said Squire Higginbottom. "What size are they?"

"A size five, sir," said Timothy tentatively.

"Perfect. How much will you take for them?"

Timothy was an honest man, not one to raise the price just because he thought a customer could pay it. But these boots *were* the finest boots he had ever sold.

"Fifteen shillings, sir," said Timothy, swallowing, amazed at his own daring for naming what seemed to him a high price.

"Sold," said Squire Higginbottom, taking out his wallet. "My wife will be delighted. And at that price, I must surely order two more pairs just like them for my lovely daughters."

"Oh my, oh my," muttered Timothy as he hurriedly retrieved the boots from the window and began wrapping them carefully with tissue and tying them up with a twist. *How shall I ever be able to make two more pairs just like this?* he wondered to himself.

"Two more pairs one size smaller. I need them by Friday," the Squire said, dropping his calling card on the counter.

"Yes, sir. Yes, sir. Thank you very much, sir," said Timothy. He handed the parcel to the elegant gentleman, who swirled out of the shop.

Greatly agitated, Timothy scurried up the steps.

"Lizzie, look! I've sold the boots! For fifteen bob!"

Elizabeth smiled weakly as Timothy rushed on. "But what are we to do? Squire Higginbottom's ordered two more pairs, just the same, and he wants them in two days. I can't make even one boot that fine. What are we to do?"

"First things first, Timothy," said Elizabeth. "Go to the tanner's and buy the leather. We shall do the best we can."

So Timothy donned his hat and his worn overcoat. Stuffing one half of the money into a jar to pay the landlord and the other half deep in his pocket, he stepped out into the chilly December air. First Timothy went to the tanner's, then to the pharmacist's to buy a bit more medicine for Elizabeth. And, finally, he made a special stop at McTufty's Bakery to get her favorite apple tart.

By bedtime, Timothy had cut up the leather, picked out the eyelets, and threaded the needles in preparation for tomorrow's work. When he went to put out fresh crumpet crumbs and raspberry wine for the Little People, he was amazed to find yesterday's crumbs gone and the thimble empty. Could it be the Wee Folk? Or was it only mice? He wanted to tell Elizabeth, but she was already asleep. Exhausted from the day's excitement, he quickly fell into bed.

But Timothy did not have a restful night. He dreamed that it was morning and again he had found all his leather missing. However, this time there was no pretty pair of boots awaiting him, just a shop full of irate customers demanding their money back.

He awoke with a start as the first rays of dawn filtered through the bedroom curtain. His heart was thumping; he had to see if his nightmare had come true. What if the leather were gone and there were no new shoes either? Quietly, he slid out of bed so as not to wake Elizabeth and stole downstairs in his dressing gown.

On the bottom step, he stopped and stared. There on his workbench were two pairs of lady's boots, exactly like the first pair but one size smaller! He could hardly trust his eyes, afraid he was still dreaming.

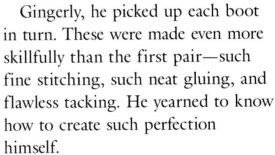

Gingerly, he picked up each boot in turn. These were made even more skillfully than the first pair—such fine stitching, such neat gluing, and flawless tacking. He yearned to know how to create such perfection himself.

The little shoemaker's shop on Limpkin Lane remained closed that day. Confident that the Squire would be delighted with his daughters' boots when he came the next day, Timothy took the rent money from the jar and strode off to the tanner's for more supplies. He returned two hours later, laden with piles of fancy suedes and kid leather—as well as a plump chicken for dinner.

All day he sat at his bench practicing his tacking and gluing, trying to match the marvelous work of his mysterious helper. Feeling well enough to join him,

Elizabeth spent the afternoon trying to duplicate
the delicacy of the tiny stitches in those marvelous boots.

As evening fell, Timothy cut up enough leather for three
new pairs of shoes and left it lying on the workbench. He
bounded upstairs for the happiest dinner he and Elizabeth
had had in many months. After the meal, he poured the usual
thimbleful of raspberry wine for the Little People, plus a
glass for himself and Elizabeth to share. As the candle
guttered low, he told her about the thimble being empty and
the crumbs gone. In bed, they sleepily wondered if it could
be an Elf or Pixie who was helping them after all? Could
their luck be turning at last? Before the candle flickered out,
however, Timothy and Elizabeth were fast asleep.

The shoemakers had high hopes when they descended the
stairs that Friday morning, and they were not disappointed.

There on the bench, in a neat little row, stood two boots and four shoes. The boots were made of carefully matched blue suede and had elegant cuffs and tassels. But the shoes! The shoes were exquisite. The kid leather Timothy had bought the day before was now embellished with the most delicate embroidery.

As Elizabeth studied one of the shoes, she suddenly exclaimed, "The twist. Timothy, look! The embroidery is done with strands of the twist we use to tie up our packages."

Soon Timothy and Elizabeth were happily practicing their stitching and tacking and gluing. They had to laugh at some of the mistakes they made but didn't let anything stop them as they kept on trying to match the mystery shoemaker's work. Just before noon, they heard three raps on the floor of the shop.

"It's Squire Higginbottom come for his daughters' shoes," cried Timothy. He jumped up from his bench, wiped his hands, straightened his apron, and practically leapt from behind the curtain to meet his customer.

But it was not Squire Higginbottom.

"Well, shoemaker," a voice growled, "I trust you are prepared for a change of quarters." It was Landlord Whipsnade, accompanied by his sniveling clerk, Edgar Smolet, and a constable.

"The money," snarled Whipsnade. "Now! And if you don't have it, I am pleased to inform you that you are hereby evicted from these premises."

"But . . ." Timothy tried to interrupt.

"You don't need to worry about where you and your dear wife will sleep tonight. We've arranged for some nice hard cots in debtors' prison. Isn't that right, Constable?" He turned to the policeman, who nodded sorrowfully.

"But I can pay," said Timothy stoutly.

"So you've told me before," snapped Whipsnade. "But I'm fed up with your promises. Constable, arrest him!"

"Sir," said the constable to Timothy, "if you do indeed have the money you owe this gentleman, please let us see it."

Now Timothy was in a bad spot. He had spent all but threepence of the money Squire Higginbottom had given him, fully expecting the Squire to pay him thirty shillings today for his daughters' boots. But the Squire hadn't come yet.

"Well, you see, sir," Timothy stammered, "I . . . I don't exactly have all the money now but I will . . . I will later today when . . ."

"Enough!" shouted Whipsnade. "Edgar, start the inventory! Those silly shoes in the window should fetch enough to cover at least part of what I'm owed."

The nearsighted clerk began shuffling around the shop, making a list of everything he could find, starting with the three exquisite new pairs that Timothy had placed in the window that morning.

Having overheard the landlord's harsh words, Elizabeth peered out from behind the workshop curtain.

"Oh, Lizzie," cried Timothy, "we're ruined."

Elizabeth's chin went up, and she said to the landlord stoutly, "You'll have your money any minute. The Squire will be here soon."

"Soon is not enough," sneered Whipsnade. "I look forward to being rid of you both!" And turning to his clerk, who stood watching open-mouthed, he shouted, "Get on with it, Edgar!"

"All is lost," despaired Timothy. "I knew our good fortune couldn't last. Let's go up and gather our things."

"It's all right," Elizabeth said. She tried to comfort him as they retreated upstairs. "Look how much we've learned this week. We'll get a new start somewhere else."

"Yes, in the workhouse," cackled Whipsnade.

Half an hour later, the clerk had finished toting up every tool in the workroom. He had just begun to list the pieces of leather tacked to the wall when the Squire entered the shop. He was accompanied by a handsomely dressed gentleman and lady. Whipsnade sprang to his feet and bowed low.

"Squire Higginbottom," Whipsnade said, groveling, "what on earth brings you to this lowly establishment?"

"Why, what else but to purchase some of the finest shoes in England!" And indicating his companions, he said, "Let me introduce my dear friends, Lord and Lady Snuffington. Master Whipsnade."

"Delighted, I'm sure," said his Lordship without the least interest. Lady Snuffington nodded imperiously.

"But where's shoemaker Sparks?" Higginbottom went on before the astonished Whipsnade could say another word.

"Ah, there you are, my good man! And this must be Mrs. Sparks!" he cried out cheerily as Timothy and Elizabeth

appeared from behind the curtain. The couple had been
packing the last of their scant belongings when they heard
voices below.

"Oh, sir, I thought perhaps you'd changed your mind,"
said Timothy.

"Changed my mind? Changed my mind? That's a good
one, eh, Leslie?" Higginbottom said to Lord Snuffington.
"Why, I not only want the boots I ordered, but I've brought
you two more clients. And if I'm not mistaken, Lord
Snuffington has already taken a fancy to those handsome blue
boots in the window."

And so the rent was paid in full and Whipsnade was
forced to apologize profusely. He even ordered a pair of
dancing shoes for himself. Lord and Lady Snuffington
ordered many more pairs of stylish shoes and warmly
recommended Timothy and Elizabeth's shop to their friends.
Sparks' Shoeshop soon became a very busy place.

Every evening for the next few weeks, Timothy and Elizabeth would lay out cut leather on the workbench, and every morning they would find a new assortment of wonderful shoes and boots mysteriously assembled. The rest of the time they practiced, practiced, practiced new methods for making shoes. But nothing they made was quite as good as the magical work they found each morning.

They were sure now that it was one of the Wee Folk who was the mysterious shoemaker. Elizabeth kept looking behind curtains and under pots hoping to find an Elf or a Pixie, but, as Timothy reminded her, Elves don't like to be seen and might be angry and make mischief if she didn't stop. But each day her curiosity grew, and soon even Timothy was beginning to peer quickly into dark corners hoping to catch a glimpse.

One afternoon just before the New Year, Elizabeth announced, "Timothy, I think we've done it! Look at this shoe!" and she held up a charming little boot that she and Timothy had made. Even the Wee Folk couldn't have made a better shoe. They laughed and clasped hands and danced for joy around the shop.

"Tim, Tim," said Elizabeth, gasping for breath, "stop a moment."

Timothy stopped leaping about, and Elizabeth said seriously, "You know how curious we are. Now that we can make the shoes ourselves, let's take a chance. We'll hide ourselves tonight under that pile of leather. We surely won't be seen there, and we will know at last who has been so kind to us."

So late that evening, Elizabeth and Timothy crept downstairs. They extinguished the candle and, covering themselves with leather, waited for the mystery shoemaker. About midnight, Timothy's head had just begun to nod when he heard what at first sounded like tiny bells ringing.

He peeked out, and there leaping about on the bench were two tiny spindly, greenish creatures—practically naked. The Little People! Elves! Timothy rubbed his eyes and leaned closer. The two had just finished sharing the raspberry wine and biscuit crumbs. Chattering rapidly to each other, they set to work.

Elizabeth too peered from under the leather. She was amazed at how quickly their nimble hands fastened, glued, hammered, and stitched. The whole time they babbled on to each other.

"Oh so nice, so very nice.
Little boots for snow and ice,"

rang out one as he rapped away on a boot.

"Yes, oh yes, so very sweet.
For a lady's dancing feet!"

tinkled the other as he stitched away on a shoe.

And giggles chimed out as they whizzed through their work. The two Elves kept on like this until the sound of sleighs going by outside had long stopped. Both Timothy and Elizabeth fell asleep where they sat hidden. When the night watchman called out four o'clock, they woke, stiff-limbed, and discovered that the Little People had gone.

The next morning, Elizabeth said, "Those clever Elves have saved us from poverty and prison and taught us a new way of working. Surely they won't mind if we give them something in return. It is such a cold winter, perhaps they would like some clothes to keep warm."

So Elizabeth made two tiny sets of clothes and Timothy made two teeny, tiny pairs of boots. That night, instead of leather cuttings, they carefully laid the clothes and shoes upon the bench and sat up to watch for the Elves.

At midnight, the Elves came skipping in looking for what work there was to be done. One of them tinkled,

"There is no leather, tack, or glue.
How will we make a lovely shoe?"

Then they discovered the miniature garments and danced about delightedly. With much fumbling and giggling they dressed themselves. After strutting about admiring themselves for a few moments, one Elf looked at the other and suddenly tinkled,

"Oh, dear! Oh, dear! Oh, dear! I fear
They must have seen us working here!"

And in a twinkling, the Elves jumped up to the window ledge and leapt through the window onto the snowy street below.

And as they jigged off arm in arm, Elizabeth and Timothy could hear them sing out,

"Now that our work at last is through,
We'll never make another shoe!"

And they disappeared around the corner at the end of Limpkin Lane.

Even though Timothy continued to put out the raspberry wine and biscuit crumbs, the Elves never came again, at least as far as the Sparkses knew. But Timothy and Elizabeth never regretted that their generosity had caused the Elves to run away, and their little business continued to prosper.

The couple worked diligently to complete their many orders for shoes and had good reason to be proud of their work. At Squire Higginbottom's glittering New Year's Eve ball, all of

the most fashionable ladies and gentlemen wore shoes from Sparks' Shoeshop.

While the Squire's guests waltzed in the New Year up on the hilltop, Timothy and Elizabeth celebrated happily in their own dear little home.

31

And for those who believed in them, the Elves were heard
to say:

"Let this New Year be fully blessed
With love and work and happiness!"